Fairy Tales
IN CROSS STITCH

Christina Marsh

MEREHURST

THE CHARTS

Some of the designs in this book are very detailed and due to inevitable
space limitations, the charts may be shown on a comparatively small
scale; in such cases, readers may find it helpful to have the particular
chart with which they are currently working enlarged.

THREADS

The projects in this book were all stitched with Anchor stranded cotton
embroidery threads. The keys given with each chart also list thread
combinations for those who wish to use DMC or Madeira threads.
It should be pointed out that the shades produced by different
companies vary slightly, and it is not always possible to find
identical colours in a different range.

First published in 1996 by Merehurst Limited
Ferry House, 51-57 Lacy Road, Putney, London SW15 1PR
Copyright © 1996 Merehurst Limited
ISBN 1 85391 521 1

A catalogue record for this book is available from the British Library.

Edited by Diana Lodge
Designed by Maggie Aldred
Photography by Juliet Piddington
Illustrations by John Hutchinson
Typesetting by Dacorum Type & Print, Hemel Hempstead
Colour separation by Fotographics Limited, UK – Hong Kong
Printed in Hong Kong by Wing King Tong

*Merehurst is the leading publisher of craft books and has an excellent range
of titles to suit all levels. Please send to the address above for our
free catalogue, stating the title of this book.*

CONTENTS

INTRODUCTION

There can be no greater cross-stitching pleasure than to embroider gifts for a child. This book contains eight projects, including plenty of cross stitch designs that will give hours of enjoyment to both the stitcher and the recipient.

The projects have been chosen to cover a wide age range, from cradle to school. Stitch picture frames to show off your favourite snap shots, or birthday cards that can double as miniature pictures when framed. Create finger puppets that bring to life the story of Little Red Riding Hood and watch your child grow with the Jack and the Bean Stalk measuring chart. Make the re-usable party crackers, and add extra magic to birthday parties and Christmas treats. Finally, send your child off to school with fun items that no child will want to be without. Stitch these and a host of other ideas that will bring a smile to any young face.

You can, of course, mix and match many of the projects. The bookmark baddies, containing all the characters that children love to hate, is the ideal small present for birthday and Hallowe'en parties. You could, however, take the Piper from the Story Book Picture and turn the design into a brightly-coloured bookmark. You might use the characters in this design for cards or miniature pictures, and practically all the designs could be stitched on bed-linen or clothes, with the aid of the waste canvas technique.

Whether you are newcomer to cross stitch or a skilled embroiderer, I am sure you will enjoy stitching these fun projects for your family or those of friends.

BASIC SKILLS

■

BEFORE YOU BEGIN

PREPARING THE FABRIC
Even with an average amount of handling, many evenweave fabrics tend to fray at the edges, so it is a good idea to overcast the raw edges, using ordinary sewing thread, before you begin.

FABRIC
The projects in this book use Aida fabric, which is ideal both for beginners and more advanced stitchers as it has a surface of clearly designated squares. All Aida fabric has a count, which refers to the number of squares (each stitch covers one square) to one inch (2.5cm); the higher the count, the smaller the finished stitching. Projects in this book use 11-, and 14- and 18- count Aida, popular and readily available sizes, in a wide variety of colours.

THE INSTRUCTIONS
Each project begins with a full list of the materials that you will require. The measurements given for the embroidery fabric include a minimum of 5cm (2in) all around to allow for stretching it in a frame and preparing the edges to prevent them from fraying.

Colour keys for stranded embroidery cottons – Anchor, DMC, or Madeira – are given with each chart. It is assumed that you will need to buy one skein of each colour mentioned in a particular key, even though you may use less, but where two or more skeins are needed, this information is included in the main list of requirements.

Before you begin to embroider, always mark the centre of the design with two lines of basting stitches, one vertical and one horizontal, running from edge to edge of the fabric, as indicated by the arrows on the charts.

As you stitch, use the centre lines given on the chart and the basting threads on your fabric as reference points for counting the squares and threads to position your design accurately.

WORKING IN A HOOP

A hoop is the most popular frame for use with small areas of embroidery. It consists of two rings, one fitted inside the other; the outer ring usually has an adjustable screw attachment so that it can be tightened to hold the stretched fabric in place. Hoops are available in several sizes, ranging from 10cm (4in) in diameter to quilting hoops with a diameter of 38cm (15in). Hoops with table stands or floor stands attached are also available.

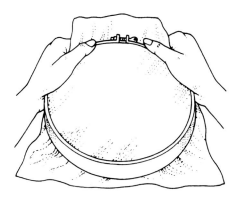

1 To stretch your fabric in a hoop, place the area to be embroidered over the inner ring and press the outer ring over it, with the tension screw released. Tissue paper can be placed between the outer ring and the embroidery, so that the hoop does not mark the fabric. Lay the tissue paper over the fabric when you set it in the hoop, then tear away the central embroidery area.

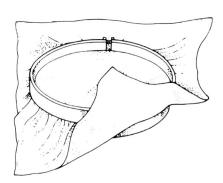

2 Smooth the fabric and, if necessary, straighten the grain before tightening the screw. The fabric should be evenly stretched.

WORKING IN A RECTANGULAR FRAME

Rectangular frames are more suitable for larger pieces of embroidery. They consist of two rollers, with tapes attached, and two flat side pieces, which slot into the rollers and are held in place by pegs or screw attachments. Available in different sizes, either alone or with adjustable table or floor stands, frames are measured by the length of the roller tape, and range in size from 30cm (12in) to 68cm (27in).

As alternatives to a slate frame, canvas stretchers and the backs of old picture frames can be used. Provided there is sufficient extra fabric around the finished size of the embroidery, the edges can be turned under and simply attached with drawing pins (thumb tacks) or staples.

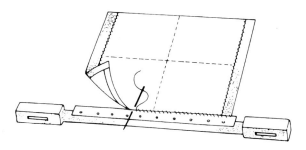

1 To stretch your fabric in a rectangular frame, cut out the fabric, allowing at least an extra 5cm (2in) all around the finished size of the embroidery. Baste a single 12mm ($\frac{1}{2}$in) turning on the top and bottom edges and oversew strong tape, 2.5cm (1in) wide, to the other two sides. Mark the centre line both ways with basting stitches. Working from the centre outward and using strong thread, oversew the top and bottom edges to the roller tapes. Fit the side pieces into the slots, and roll any extra fabric on one roller until the fabric is taut.

2 Insert the pegs or adjust the screw attachments to secure the frame. Thread a large-eyed needle (chenille needle) with strong thread or fine string and lace both edges, securing the ends around the intersections of the frame. Lace the webbing at 2.5cm (1in) intervals, stretching the fabric evenly.

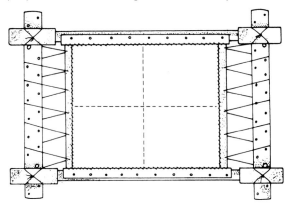

EXTENDING EMBROIDERY FABRIC

It is easy to extend a piece of embroidery fabric, such as a bookmark, to stretch it in a hoop.

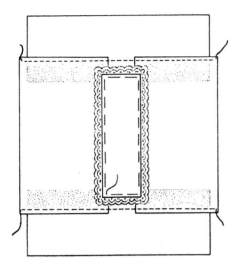

● Fabric oddments of a similar weight can be used. Simply cut four pieces to size (in other words, to the measurement that will fit both the embroidery fabric and your hoop) and baste them to each side of the embroidery fabric before stretching it in the hoop in the usual way.

THE STITCHES

CROSS STITCH

For all cross stitch embroidery, the following two methods of working are used. In each case, neat rows of vertical stitches are produced on the back of the fabric.

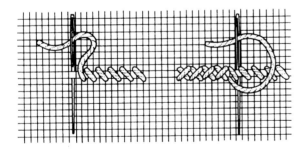

● When stitching large areas, work in horizontal rows. Working from right to left, complete the first row of evenly spaced diagonal stitches over the number of threads specified in the project instructions. Then, working from left to right, repeat the process. Continue in this way, making sure each stitch crosses in the same direction.

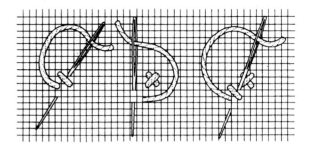

● When stitching diagonal lines, work downwards, completing each stitch before moving to the next. When starting a project always begin to embroider at the centre of the design and work outwards to ensure that the design will be placed centrally on the fabric.

BACKSTITCH

Backstitch is used in the projects to give emphasis to a particular foldline, an outline or a shadow. The stitches are worked over the same number of threads as the cross stitch, forming continuous straight or diagonal lines.

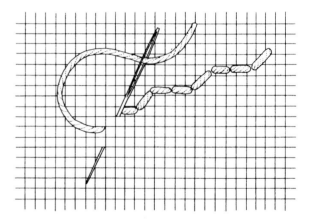

● Make the first stitch from left to right; pass the needle behind the fabric and bring it out one stitch length ahead to the left. Repeat and continue in this way along the line.

THREE-QUARTER CROSS STITCHES

Some fractional stitches are used on certain projects in this book; although they strike fear into the hearts of less experienced stitchers they are not difficult to master, and give a more natural line in certain instances. Should you find it difficult to pierce the centre of the Aida block, simply use a sharp needle to make a small hole in the centre first.

To work a three-quarter cross, bring the needle up

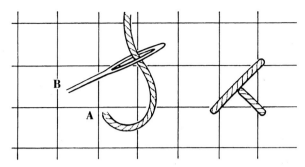
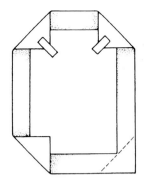

at point A and down through the centre of the square at B. Later, the diagonal back stitch finishes the stitch. A chart square with two different symbols separated by a diagonal line requires two 'three-quarter' stitches. Backstitch will later finish the square.

FRENCH KNOTS
This stitch is shown on some of the diagrams by a small circle. Where there are several french knots, the circles have been omitted to avoid confusion. Where this occurs you should refer to the instructions of the project, the detail chart and the colour photograph.

To work a french knot, bring your needle and cotton out slightly to the right of where you want your knot to be. Wind the thread once or twice around the needle, depending on how big you want your knot to be, and insert the needle to the left of the point where you brought it out.

Be careful not to pull too hard or the knot will disappear through the fabric. The instructions state the number of strands of cotton to be used for the french knots.

FINISHING

MOUNTING EMBROIDERY
The cardboard should be cut to the size of the finished embroidery, with an extra amount added all round to allow for the recess in the frame.

LIGHTWEIGHT FABRICS

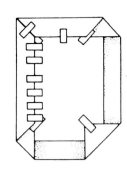

1 Place embroidery face down, with the cardboard centred on top, and basting and pencil lines matching. Begin by folding over the fabric at each corner and securing it with masking tape.

2 Working first on one side and then the other, fold over the fabric on all sides and secure it firmly with pieces of masking tape, placed about 2.5cm (1in) apart. Also neaten the mitred corners with masking tape, pulling the fabric tightly to give a firm, smooth finish.

HEAVIER FABRICS

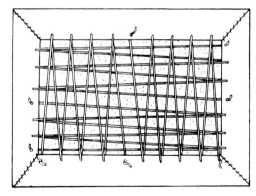

● Lay the embroidery face down, with the cardboard centred on top; fold over the edges of the fabric on opposite sides, making mitred folds at the corners, and lace across, using strong thread. Repeat on the other two sides. Finally, pull up the fabric firmly over the cardboard. Overstitch the mitred corners.

Story Book Picture

Straight from the pages of a story book come Cinderella and her Ugly Sisters, Snow White and the seven dwarfs, Sleeping Beauty and the Pied Piper – a band of friends guaranteed to dance in and out of the dreams of any child.

STORY BOOK PICTURE

YOU WILL NEED

For the picture, set in a frame with an aperture measuring 29cm × 24cm (11½in × 9½in):

40cm × 35cm (16in × 14in) of cream, 11-count Aida fabric
Stranded embroidery cotton in the colours given in the panel
No24 tapestry needle
A frame with an aperture as specified above
Firm card to fit the frame
Lightweight synthetic batting/wadding, the same size as the card
Strong thread and cardboard, for mounting
Glue stick

●

THE EMBROIDERY

Prepare the fabric (see page 4), and mark horizontal and vertical centre lines with basting stitches in a light-coloured thread. Mount the fabric in a frame (see page 5) and start the design from the centre.

Following the chart, complete all the cross stitching first, using two strands of thread in the needle. These designs contain three-quarter stitches (see page 6), which are shown on the chart by the smaller symbols, and should be stitched in the corners indicated. Be careful not to take dark threads across the back of the work in such a way that they show through on the right side. Backstitch the outline, using one strand of navy blue thread. Finally, stitch the stars with one strand of navy blue thread in the needle; stitch one long single line for each of the sides of the stars.

FINISHING

Remove the embroidery from the frame and wash if necessary, then press lightly on the wrong side, using a steam iron. Spread glue evenly on one side of the mounting card, and lightly press the batting (wadding) to the surface. Lace the embroidery over the padded surface (see page 7), using the basting stitches (if any) to check that the embroidery is centred over the card.

Remove basting stitches; place the mounted embroidery in the frame, and assemble the frame according to the manufacturer's instuctions.

STORY BOOK PICTURE		ANCHOR	DMC	MADEIRA			ANCHOR	DMC	MADEIRA
⊟	White	1	White	White	◇	Pale lilac	108	210	0802
⟋	Pale yellow	301	744	0110	◆	Medium lilac	111	208	0804
↑	Yellow beige	307	783	2212	⊟	Brown	371	433	2303
·	Pale peach	8	353	0304	☐	Pinky red	39	309	0507
⠒⠒	Medium peach	9	352	0303		Navy blue*	127	939	1009
V	Apple green	241	703	1401					
▲	Medium green	210	367	1312					
◯	Powder blue	144	800	1002	*Note: backstitch outline and stars in navy blue* (used for backstitching				
●	Medium blue	145	799	1004	only), using one strand of thread in the needle.				

Red Riding Hood Finger Puppets

Stitch these colourful finger puppets
and bring to life a favourite story.
This charming set would be an ideal
gift to bring some drama and
excitement to a convalescent child.

RED RIDING HOOD FINGER PUPPETS

YOU WILL NEED

For six finger puppets, each measuring approximately 7.5cm × 4cm (3in × 1½in):

40cm × 20cm (16in × 8in) of white, 14-count Aida fabric
40cm × 20cm (16in × 8in) of cotton fabric
Stranded embroidery cotton in the colours given in the panel
No26 tapestry needle
Sewing cotton to match fabric

●

THE EMBROIDERY

Using a light-coloured thread, baste six boxes, each with a count of twenty horizontal squares by eighty vertical squares. Position the boxes side by side, as shown in the diagram, with an allowance of five squares between each. Mount the Aida fabric in a hoop or frame (see pages 4 and 5). If you wish to work in a hoop, you may need a larger piece of Aida fabric or additional strips to increase the size of the fabric.

Embroider one figure in each of the six boxes, placing each design in the top forty squares of a rectangular box. Following the appropriate chart, complete all the cross stitching, using two strands of thread in the needle. These designs contain three-quarter stitches (see page 6) which are shown on the chart by the smaller symbols; and should be stitched in the corners indicated. Do not take threads from one design to another as the stitching may unravel when the embroideries are separated. Backstitch the eyes with three strands of navy thread in the needle; alternatively you may prefer to use french knots. The main outline of each design should be backstitched with one strand of navy thread.

MAKING THE FINGER PUPPETS

Take the finished embroidery from the frame; wash if necessary, and press lightly with a steam iron. Do not remove the basting stitches around the boxes as these will be used as guide lines for the machining. Place the cotton backing fabric and the Aida together, right sides facing, and pin around the perimeter.

Machine around three sides of each puppet (two sides and the top), leaving the bottom unstitched; to do this, use the basting stitches as guidelines, and machine outside the boxes, approximately one square away from the basted line. Machine around all six boxes before dividing the puppets.

To separate, cut between the stitched puppets, taking care not to trim too close to the stitching. Trim away any surplus material and overlock the edges to prevent fraying.

Turn the puppets inside out. This will need to be done very carefully – try not to pull on the embroideries. You will find a blunt object, such as the end of a pen, useful for pushing out the corners. Remove any creases by pressing, then overlock the open end. Finally, push the overlocked end up and into the top to form the lining.

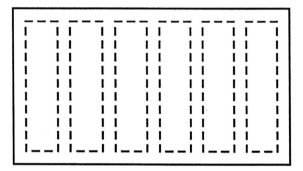

Marking out the embroidery fabric

RED RIDING HOOD FINGER PUPPETS ▶		ANCHOR	DMC	MADEIRA
╱	Yellow	305	743	0113
▲	Orange	303	741	0114
·	Pale peach	6	754	0304
∷	Medium peach	9	353	0303
◎	Red	335	606	0209
☒	Green	255	907	1410
◇	Blue	145	799	1003
●	Brown	359	898	2006
─	Grey	848	928	1708
	Navy blue*	150	823	1008

Note: backstitch the outline around each design in navy blue* (used for backstitching only), and stitch the mouths of Red Riding Hood, Grandma and the Woodcutter in red, using one strand in the needle.

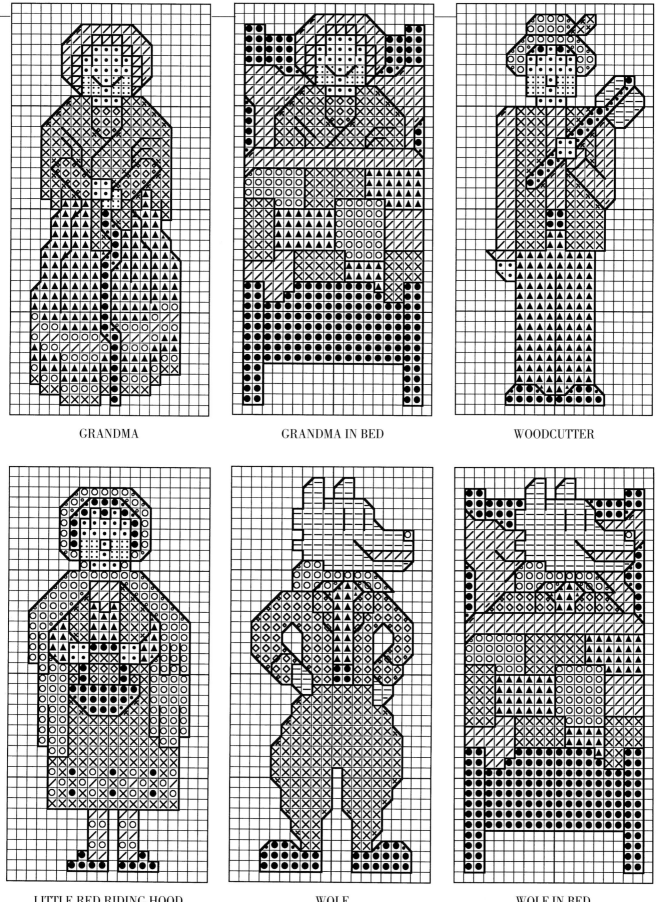

GRANDMA

GRANDMA IN BED

WOODCUTTER

LITTLE RED RIDING HOOD

WOLF

WOLF IN BED

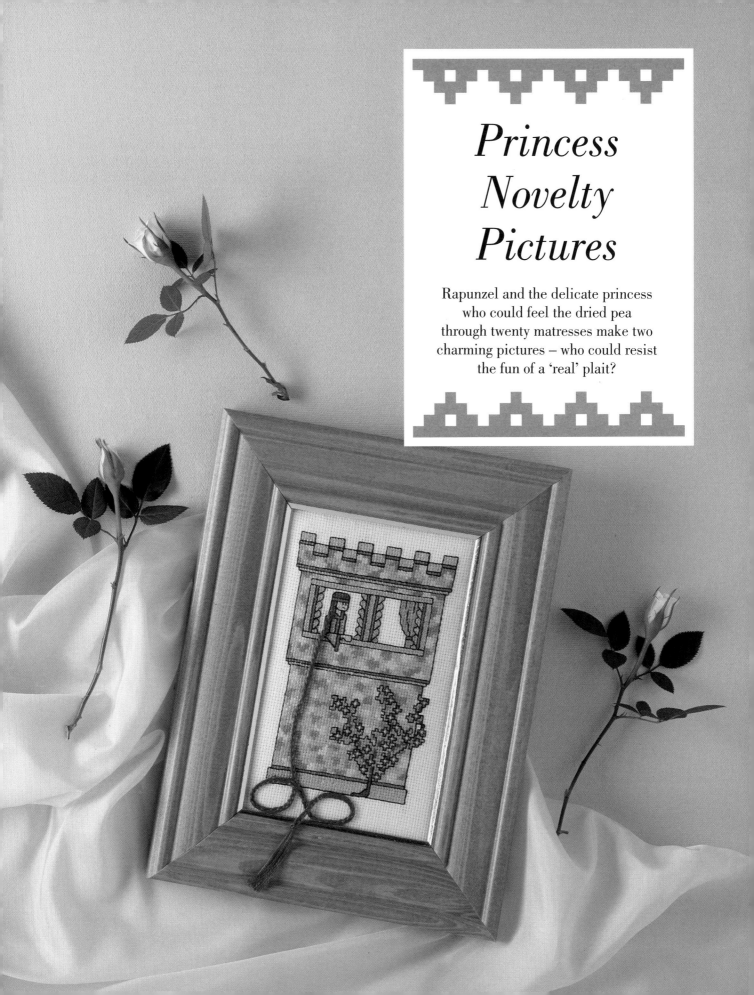

Princess Novelty Pictures

Rapunzel and the delicate princess who could feel the dried pea through twenty matresses make two charming pictures – who could resist the fun of a 'real' plait?

PRINCESS NOVELTY PICTURES

YOU WILL NEED

For each picture set in a frame with an internal measurement of 8.5cm × 13.5cm (3½in × 5½in):

25cm × 20cm (10in × 8in) of white, 18-count
Aida fabric
No26 tapestry needle
Stranded embroidery cotton in the colours given
in the panel
Picture frame as specified above
Firm card to fit the frame

Lightweight synthetic batting/wadding,
the same size as the card
Strong thread for mounting
Glue stick

Note: the same thread colours are used for both pictures; if you wish to embroider both designs, finish one picture and then decide whether you need any additional skeins before you start the next.

•

THE EMBROIDERY

Prepare the fabric as described on page 4; find the centre by folding the fabric in half and then in half again, and lightly pressing the folded corner, or by marking the horizontal and vertical centre lines with basting stitches in a light-coloured thread. Mount

the fabric in a frame (see page 5), and start the design from the centre.

Following the chart, complete all the cross stitching first, using one strand of thread in the needle. These designs contain three-quarter stitches (see page 6), which are shown on the chart by the smaller symbols, and should be stitched in the corners indicated. Finish with the backstitching, again using one strand of thread. In the Princess picture, create the pea in the palm of her hand with one French knot, using three strands of thread in the needle.

Cut three lengths of medium brown thread approximately 30cm (12in) long. Knot the ends, and stitch each thread through the fabric at the base of the hair so that the knot is at the back of the work. Plait the threads: take the right-hand thread up and over the

middle thread, which now becomes the middle thread; next, take the left-hand thread up and over the middle thread. By repeating this operation, plait to the end of the threads, then secure the ends by knotting.

MOUNTING AND FRAMING

Remove the finished embroidery from the frame and wash if necessary, then press lightly on the wrong side, using a steam iron. Spread glue evenly on one side of the mounting card and lightly press the batting/wadding to the surface. Lace the embroidery over the padded surface (see page 7), using the basting stitches (if any) to check that the embroidery is centred over the card. Remove basting stitches; coil the hair at the bottom of the picture, and place the mounted embroidery in the frame according to the manufacturer's instructions.

PRINCESS NOVELTY PICTURES ◄		ANCHOR	DMC	MADEIRA
·	Lemon yellow	301	744	0110
∷	Pale peach	8	754	0304
Z	Medium peach	9	352	0302
O	Deep pink	39	309	0507
□	Pale blue	160	813	1002
●	Medium blue	146	798	0911
	Dark blue*	150	823	1007
V	Grass green	225	703	1307
⊡	Light brown	349	301	2306
▲	Medium brown	358	433	2008

Note: backstitch the outline with one strand of dark blue thread* (used for backstitching only).

Jack and the Beanstalk

Stitch this chart and watch your
child grow up to the giant's castle.
The chart reaches 100cm (39³⁄₈in),
but you could change the
measurements for an older child.

JACK AND THE
BEANSTALK

YOU WILL NEED

For the wall chart, measuring 69cm × 15cm
(27in × 6in) approximately:

*78.5cm × 22.5cm (31in × 9in) of cream,
11-count Aida fabric
74cm × 20cm (29in × 8in) of cream cotton
fabric, for backing,
Stranded cottons in the colours given in the
appropriate panel
No24 tapestry needle
Cream sewing cotton
Wall hanging rods for a hanging 15cm (6in) wide,
for suppliers see page 40*

THE EMBROIDERY

Prepare the fabric as described on page 4; find the centre by folding the fabric in half and then in half again, and lightly pressing the folded corner, or by marking the horizontal and vertical centre lines with basting stitches in a light-coloured thread. Mount the fabric in a frame (see page 5) and start the embroidery by stitching the measurements on the left-hand side of the design. These must be stitched carefully as the number of squares between the marks changes at 10cm intervals; this is an adjustment to improve the accuracy of the measurement chart.

Following the chart, complete the measurement marks first, using three strands of thread in the needle. Continue with the cross-stitching, again using three strands of thread in the needle. This design contains three-quarter stitches (see page 6), which are shown on the chart by the smaller symbols, and should be stitched in the corners indicated. Be care-

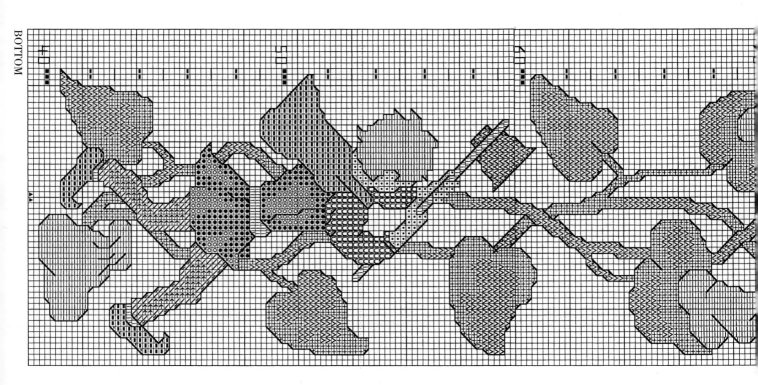

BOTTOM

ful not to take dark threads across the back of the work in such a way that they show through on the right side. Backstitch the outline, using two strands of navy blue in the needle.

MAKING THE HANGING

Remove the finished embroidery from the frame and wash if necessary, then press lightly on the wrong side, using a steam iron. Keeping the embroidery centred, trim the Aida fabric to the same measurement as the backing fabric. Place the embroidery and backing fabric with right sides together and pin. Baste and then machine stitch down the length of the fabric on each side (you should have an allowance of five clear squares down each side between the stitching line and the embroidered area). Turn the work right side out and press.

To make the folds for the bell pull, overlock the Aida and backing fabric together at each end. Make a 2.5cm (1in) turning to the back of the work at both the top and bottom of the hanging. Machine stitch the hem approximately 6mm (¼in) from the turned edge. Insert the rods and assemble according to the manufacturer's instructions.

JACK AND THE BEANSTALK		ANCHOR	DMC	MADEIRA
V	Grey	848	927	1708
Y	Medium rose	68	3688	0604
⌐	Deep rose	69	3687	0603
☐	Light blue	161	826	1012
▣	Medium blue	162	825	1011
	Navy blue*	150	823	1008
←	Pale orange	302	743	0113
＼	Orange	303	742	0114
−	Bronze	309	781	2009
▯	Medium brown	357	801	2302
·	Peach	6	754	0305
▬	Red	13	349	0212
U	Light lilac	108	210	0801
⬭	Medium lilac	98	553	0803
●	Medium purple	111	208	0804
⋀	Light green	226	702	1306
＋	Medium green	230	910	1301

Note: where small symbol is shown, work a three-quarter stitch in the corner indicated; backstitch around the outline with two strands of navy blue* (used for backstitching only).

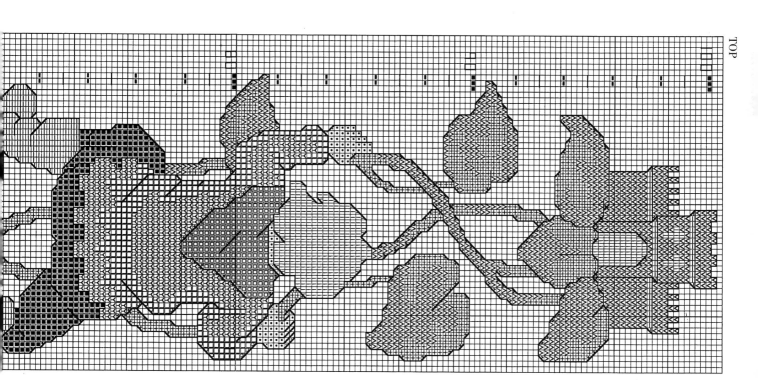

Fairy Tale Cards

Fun to stitch and a joy to receive, a card is a lovely gift to make a child feel special. You could use any of these attractive designs for a birthday, a 'get well' token, or perhaps just to send your love to a faraway grandchild.

FAIRY TALE CARDS

YOU WILL NEED

For each design, set in a card with an oval aperture measuring 12.5cm x 9cm (5in × 3¹⁄₂in):

*17.5cm × 12.5cm (7in × 5in) of cream,
14-count Aida fabric
Stranded embroidery cotton in the colours given
in the appropriate panel
No26 tapestry needle
Card with an aperture as specified above,
for suppliers see page 40*

•

THE EMBROIDERY

Prepare the fabric as described on page 4; find the centre by folding the fabric in half and then in half again, and lightly pressing the folded corner, or by marking the horizontal and vertical lines with basting stitches in a light-coloured thread. Mount the fabric in a hoop (see page 4) and start the embroidery at the centre of the design.

Following the chart, complete all the cross-stitching, using two strands of thread in the needle. These designs contains three-quarter stitches (see page 6), which are shown on the chart by the smaller symbols, and should be stitched in the corners indicated. Backstitch the outline, using one strand of navy blue thread. For the elf picture, stitch the needle with two strands of thread, and for his sewing cotton attach one strand of thread to the top of the boot and the bottom of the needle.

MOUNTING AND FRAMING

Remove the finished embroidery from the frame and remove any basting stitches. Wash if necessary, then press lightly on the wrong side, using a steam iron. Keeping the design centred, trim the embroidery to measure about 12mm (¹⁄₂in) larger all around than the size of the card window. Position the embroidery behind the window; open out the self-adhesive mount; fold the card, and press firmly to secure it. Some cards require a dab of glue to ensure a secure and neat finish.

SLEEPING BEAUTY ▶	ANCHOR	DMC	MADEIRA
⧄ Pale orange	302	743	0113
· Pale peach	8	353	0304
⠘ Medium peach	9	352	0303
▬ Red	46	666	0210
◇ Medium brown	349	3776	2310
‖ Medium green	226	702	1306
✕ Purple	111	552	0713
● Royal blue	133	796	0913
◼ Navy blue	127	939	1009

Note: backstitch around the outline, using one strand of navy blue thread in the needle.

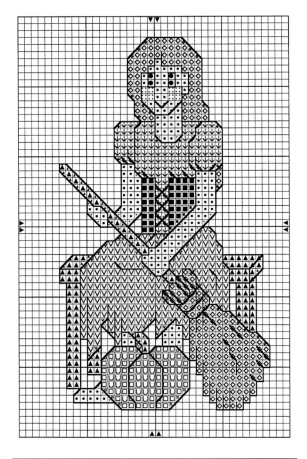

CINDERELLA ▲	ANCHOR	DMC	MADEIRA
· Pale peach	8	353	0304
⠘ Medium peach	9	352	0303
U Medium orange	303	742	0114
▢ Deep orange	304	741	0202
◇ Medium brown	349	3776	2310
▲ Warm brown	352	300	2304
↓ Grass green	255	907	1410
V Lilac	98	553	0712
● Royal blue	133	796	0913
◼ Navy blue*	127	939	1009

Note: backstitch around the outline, using one strand of navy blue thread (used for backstitching only) in the needle.*

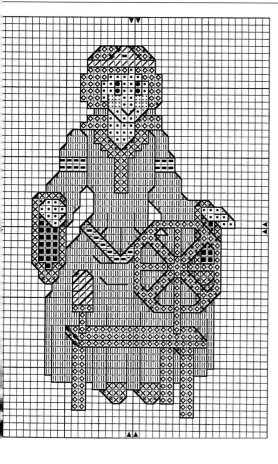

PUSS IN BOOTS ▼		ANCHOR	DMC	MADEIRA
Y	White	1	White	White
⁄	Pale orange	302	743	0113
⟍	Light brown	347	436	2309
◇	Medium brown	349	3776	2310
◆	Dark brown	357	801	2007
−	Red	46	666	0210
↓	Grass green	255	907	1410
▽	Emerald green	228	700	1304
∣	Light blue	145	799	0910
●	Royal blue	133	796	0913
	Navy blue*	127	939	1009

Note: backstitch around the outline, using one strand of navy blue thread* (used for backstitching only) in the needle.

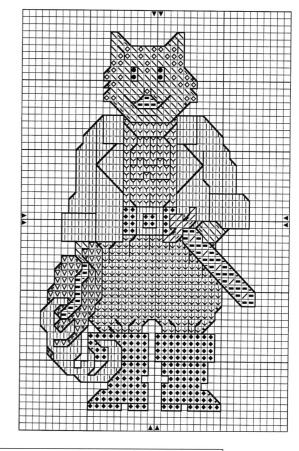

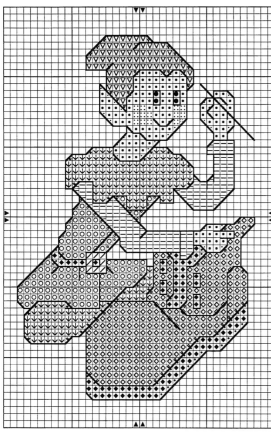

THE ELVES AND THE SHOE MAKER ◄		ANCHOR	DMC	MADEIRA
·	Pale peach	8	353	0304
∷	Medium peach	9	352	0303
⁄	Pale orange	302	743	0113
○	Pinky red	39	309	0507
−	Yellow green	279	734	1610
↓	Grass green	255	907	1410
▽	Emerald green	228	700	1304
◇	Medium brown	349	3776	2310
◆	Dark brown	357	801	2007
●	Royal blue	133	796	0913
	Navy blue*	127	939	1009

Note: backstitch around the outline, using one strand of navy blue thread* (used for backstitching only) in the needle.

Snow White Party Crackers

Filled with a cracker and a small gift of your choice, these are ideal for children's birthday parties or Christmas treats, and if you wash them carefully, they can be re-used.

SNOW WHITE PARTY CRACKERS

YOU WILL NEED

For the complete set of eight crackers:

One sheet of 10-count plastic canvas
Stranded embroidery cotton in the colours given
in the panel
No24 tapestry needle
50cm (½yd) of cotton fabric, 90cm (1yd) wide, in
each of two contrasting colours
Sewing threads to match the fabrics and the
zigzag braid (see below)
50cm (½yd) of interfacing (pelmet weight)
80cm (30in) of ribbon, 2.5cm (1in) wide, in each of
two contrasting colours to match the fabrics
3.1m (3½yds) of ribbon, 3mm (⅛in) wide, in each of
the same two colours as above
1.6m (1⅔yds) of zigzag braid
1m (1yd) of iron-on Velcro, 2cm (¾in) wide
Eight cardboard tubes, each 10cm (4in) long and
4cm (1½in) in diameter (toilet roll centres are ideal)
Fillings of your choice

Note: cut the Velcro down the centre, to create two
1m (1yd) lengths.

Using the above cut, for each cracker, measuring
approximately 23.5cm in length × 4.5cm in diameter
(9¼in × 1¾in):

31.5cm × 19cm (12½in × 7½in) of cotton fabric
Interfacing – two 16cm × 5.5cm (6½in × 2¼in)
pieces, and one 16cm × 11cm (6½in × 4¼in) piece
Velcro – one 2.5cm (1in) length, two 5cm (2in)
lengths and one 10cm (4in) length
Wide ribbon – 19cm (7½in), to contrast with
the fabric
Narrow ribbon – two 38cm (15in) lengths, to
contrast with the fabric

•

THE EMBROIDERY

Work all the figures before attempting to cut the canvas, as cutting errors cannot be rectified. Remember to leave at least one space between designs for cutting. Follow the chart and cross stitch, using all six strands of thread in the needle; do not take threads from one design to another as the stitching may unravel when the motifs are separated. Finally, backstitch the eyes and mouths, again using all six strands of thread.

Cut away surplus canvas carefully, the cutting line being the first empty square around the embroidery; do not cut into an embroidered square. Each figure will be left with a plastic ridge around the perimeter; simply overcast this in the light brown thread, still using all six strands in the needle.

MAKING THE CRACKERS

For each cracker, take a piece of cotton fabric and lay a smaller-sized piece of interfacing on the right side at one end, with long edges matching and an even overlap of fabric at the sides. Taking a 6mm (¼in) allowance, machine the two together down the long edge. Bring the fabric over the interfacing (folding the fabric only to create a 6mm/¼in hem of fabric at the wrong side) and machine the two together along the other long edge. Repeat this operation at the other end of the cracker. Position the larger piece of interfacing on the centre of the fabric (wrong side), and machine along the two long edges.

Turn to the right side of the fabric, and machine a length of zigzag braid to each end, approximately 2.5cm (1in) from the folded edge. Place a contrast strip of wide ribbon across the centre of the fabric and stitch the ribbon to the fabric down each long edge, either slipstitching neatly and unobtrusively by hand or with machine stitching.

Turn a double 6mm (¼in) hem to the wrong side down each long edge of the cracker, and neatly slipstitch in place.

Separate the three longer Velcro strips and place the hooked sections on the inside edge (over the hem and interfacing); the corresponding pieces go on the outside of the fabric down the opposite edge, so that when the fabric is wrapped around the cardboard tube, the strips will interlock. Use the diagram to check that the strips are correctly placed, before ironing them in position. Finally, machine them to secure them in position.

Thread narrow ribbon into a large-eyed sharp needle and stitch it exactly in between the interfacing pieces at each side of the centre strip, to create the ribbon ties at each end of the cracker. Take the remaining, short piece of Velcro and stitch one side down the back of a canvas motif and the other section down the centre of the cracker, across the ribbon.

Place the cardboard tube, and fillings of your choice, at the centre back of the cracker; close the strips; draw up the ribbon ties; tie a bow at each end, and lightly press the motif to the centre of the cracker.

It is important to stitch the iron-on Velcro securely to the fabric and motif as young children can not be expected to handle these crackers gently. To wash the crackers, simply remove the motifs and wash in the normal way. The canvas motifs can be washed by hand but should not be ironed.

SNOW WHITE AND THE SEVEN DWARFS		ANCHOR	DMC	MADEIRA
II	Cream	275	712	2101
·	Light peach	6	754	0502
∷	Medium peach	8	353	0503
+	Gold	306	725	0113
/	Light brown	374	420	2104
Y	Medium brown	358	433	2008
■	Dark brown	381	938	2005
O	Red	46	666	0210
●	Dark red	43	816	0512
↓	Yellow green	279	734	1610
3	Grass green	255	907	1410
X	Dark green	246	986	1405
◆	Royal blue	133	796	0913

Note: stitch the eyes in royal blue and mouths in red.

RIGHT SIDE

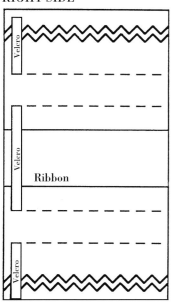

WRONG SIDE

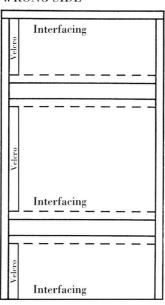

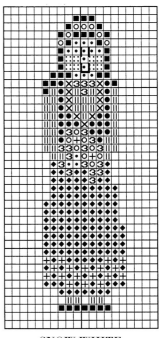

SNOW WHITE

Bookmark Baddies

Here is a set of characters that children love to hate. A hand-stitched bookmark baddy would make the perfect small token to be slipped inside a birthday card or used as a parting gift after a Hallowe'en party.

BOOKMARK BADDIES

YOU WILL NEED

For each bookmark, measuring 23cm × 5cm (9in × 2in), including the fringe:

*33cm × 22.5cm (13in × 9in) of white
14-count Aida fabric
Stranded embroidery cotton in the colours given
in the appropriate panel
No26 tapestry needle
Sewing cotton to match the fabric*

Note: one skein of each colour on the combined list is sufficient for all three designs. The fabric quantity quoted above includes an allowance of 10cm (4in) each way, for framing; if you are making more than one bookmark, allow 23cm ×12.5cm (9in × 5in) for each, plus a 5cm (2in) margin around the total area.

•

THE EMBROIDERY

Prepare the fabric as described on page 4; find the centre by folding the fabric in half and then in half again, and lightly pressing the folded corner, or by marking the horizontal and vertical centre lines with basting stitches in a light-coloured thread. If you are stitching two or more designs at once, separate the bookmark areas 23cm x 12.5cm (9in x 5in) with lines of basting stitches, and mark the centre of each area, but do not cut them apart until you have finished the embroidery. Mount the prepared fabric in a hoop or frame (see page 4 and 5).

Following the chart, complete all the cross-stitching, using two strands of thread in the needle. These designs contain three-quarter stitches (see page 6), which are shown on the chart by the smaller symbols, and should be stitched in the corners indicated. Finish with the backstitching. Use one strand of black thread in the needle for the outline. Finally, stitch the stars with two strands of golden yellow thread in the needle, making each side of each star with one long single stitch.

MAKING THE BOOKMARK

Remove the finished embroidery from the frame. If you are making several bookmarks trim away the 5cm (2in) margin around the total area, and cut the embroideries apart along the basted dividing lines; if you are making one bookmark only, trim the fabric to the correct size – 23cm × 12.5cm (9in × 5in).

Fray the top and bottom of fabric by removing horizontal threads, leaving about 2cm (³/₄in) of vertical threads showing. Oversew the fabric at the base of the frayed edges with matching sewing cotton to prevent further fraying. Fold the fabric down each side of the work to the back, leaving about 3mm (¹/₈in) clearance each side of the embroidery, and press the folds lightly with a steam iron. At the back of the work, place one flap over the other, turning in a small seam down the overlapping edge, and finish by hemming the length of the bookmark.

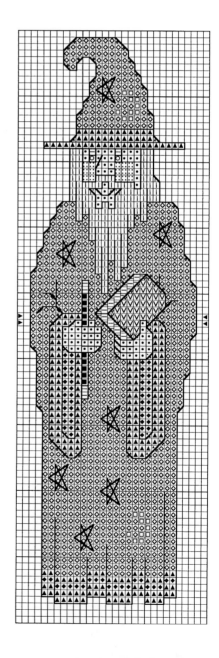

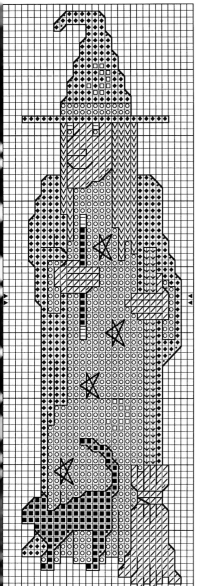

ALL THREE DESIGNS		ANCHOR	DMC	MADEIRA
⊟	White	1	White	White
⊓	Grey	397	453	1805
⊡	Golden yellow	302	743	0113
↓	Light brown	349	301	2306
·	Pale peach	6	754	0304
∷	Medium peach	9	353	0303
X	Rose red	39	309	0507
◆	Plum	69	3685	0602
◿	Apple green	240	368	1604
V	Medium green	230	910	1301
●	Dark green	862	520	1506
○	Blue	137	797	1004
◇	Lilac	98	553	0711
▲	Purple	101	550	0712
■	Black	403	Black	Black

WITCH ◀		ANCHOR	DMC	MADEIRA
⊟	White	1	White	White
⊡	Golden yellow	302	743	0113
◿	Apple green	240	368	1604
V	Medium green	230	910	1301
○	Blue	137	797	1004
◆	Plum	69	3685	0602
↓	Light brown	349	301	2306
■	Black	403	Black	Black

Note: backstitch around the outline in black and the stars in golden yellow.

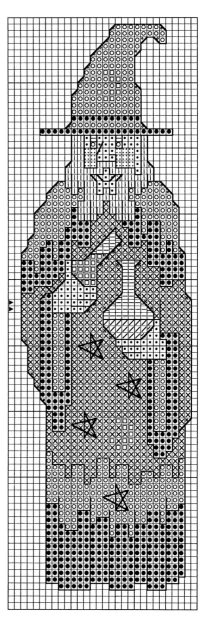

SORCERER ▶		ANCHOR	DMC	MADEIRA
⊟	White	1	White	White
⊓	Grey	397	453	1805
⊡	Golden yellow	302	743	0113
·	Pale peach	6	754	0304
∷	Medium peach	9	353	0303
X	Rose red	39	309	0507
◿	Apple green	240	368	1604
●	Dark green	862	520	1506
○	Blue	137	797	1004
■	Black	403	Black	Black

Note: backstitch around the outline in black and the stars in golden yellow.

WIZARD ◀		ANCHOR	DMC	MADEIRA
⊟	White	1	White	White
⊓	Grey	397	453	1805
⊡	Golden yellow	302	743	0113
·	Pale peach	6	754	0304
∷	Medium peach	9	353	0303
V	Medium green	230	910	1301
○	Blue	137	797	1004
◇	Lilac	98	553	0711
▲	Purple	101	550	0712
◆	Plum	69	3685	0602
■	Black	403	Black	Black

Note: backstitch around the outline in black and the stars in golden yellow.

Genie at School

This delightful set of items – a gym bag, a pencil case, and a set of little novelty designs – all based on the story of Aladdin and his wondrous lamp, would make a lovely gift to celebrate a child's first day at school, or the start of a new year.

GENIE AT SCHOOL

For the gym bag, measuring 32cm × 45.5cm
(12½in × 18in):

23cm × 12.5cm (9in × 5in) of 14-count waste canvas
Stranded embroidery cotton in the colours given
in the panel
Sharp-pointed needle
66cm × 50.5cm (26in × 20in) of lightweight denim
Matching sewing cotton
1m (1yd) of medium-weight cord

For the pencil case, measuring approximately
16cm × 12cm (6½in × 4½in):

15cm × 10cm (6in × 4in) of 14-count waste canvas
Stranded embroidery cotton in the colours
given in the panel
Sharp-pointed needle
25cm × 20cm (10in × 8in) of lightweight denim
25cm × 20cm (10in × 8in) of pelmet-weight
interfacing
Matching sewing cotton
15cm (6in) jeans zip

For three pencil-case novelties, each measuring
approximately 4.5cm × 2.5cm (1¾in × 1in):

10-count plastic canvas
Stranded embroidery cotton in the colours
given in the panel
No24 tapestry needle
Sticky-backed plastic
Strong thread, for ties

●

THE EMBROIDERY FOR GYM BAG
AND PENCIL CASE

Fold the fabric for the gym bag in half to form a rectangle measuring 33cm × 50.5cm (13in × 20in) and press. Unfold the fabric; place the waste canvas in the middle of one half of the fabric, with the fold at one side, and baste in position. For the pencil case fold the fabric in half to form a rectangle measuring 20cm × 10cm (8in × 4in) and press. Unfold the fabric; place the waste canvas in the middle of the top half of the fabric, with the fold at the bottom, and baste in position.

Mount the fabric in a frame (see page 5) and start

the design in the middle, treating each pair of canvas threads as one. Following the chart, complete all the cross stitching first, using three strands of thread in a sharp-pointed needle. Finally, backstitch around the outline, using two strands of royal blue thread in the needle.

When you have finished the embroidery cut away surplus canvas, leaving about 12mm (½in) of waste canvas around the design. Dampen the right side with slightly warm water and leave it for a few minutes until the sizing in the canvas softens. Gently remove the canvas threads, one at a time, using tweezers. The threads should come out easily, but the operation requires patience; if you try to remove several threads at once, this could spoil the embroidery. Finally, dry and press the work.

MAKING THE GYM BAG

Fold the fabric in half, with the embroidery on the inside, and pin along the opposite edge to the fold and across the bottom. Machine down the side and along the bottom, 12mm (½in) from the edge, and finish by overlocking the raw edges to stop the fabric fraying. Fold the fabric at the top of the bag over to the wrong side to form a 12mm (½in) turning and press the fold. Fold the fabric again to form a 2.5cm (1in) hem and machine along the bottom edge, leaving a 5cm (2in) opening at the seam. Insert the cord and knot the ends together. Turn the bag right side out and press to finish.

MAKING THE PENCIL CASE

Place the fabric, right side up, on the interfacing and baste together. Place the zip, face down, along the top edge of the fabric and machine in place. Place the other side of the zip on the opposite edge and machine – the work at this stage is inside out. Make sure that the zip is open before pinning, then machine down the sides of the case. Overlock the sides to stop the fabric fraying. Turn the case right side out and finish by pressing.

PENCIL CASE NOVELTIES

Following the chart, cross stitch, using six strands of thread in the needle. Do not take threads from one design to another as the stitching may unravel when the canvas is separated. Backstitch, using six strands of thread, in the background colour chosen. Trim away surplus canvas by cutting into the first set of empty holes around the design. Do not cut into embroidered holes. Overcast the plastic around the design in the background colour, using all six strands of thread. Finally, stick a small square of sticky-backed plastic on the wrong side of the canvas and carefully trim to fit shape. Attach the motif by a strong thread, laced through the top of the lamp, to the object required.

GENIE AT SCHOOL		ANCHOR	DMC	MADEIRA
•	White	1	White	White
▬	Lemon yellow	288	445	0103
X	Golden yellow	291	444	0106
○	Pink	54	956	0611
‖	Spring green	226	702	1306
●	Royal blue	133	796	0913

Note: backstitch around outline, using two strands of royal blue thread in the needle.

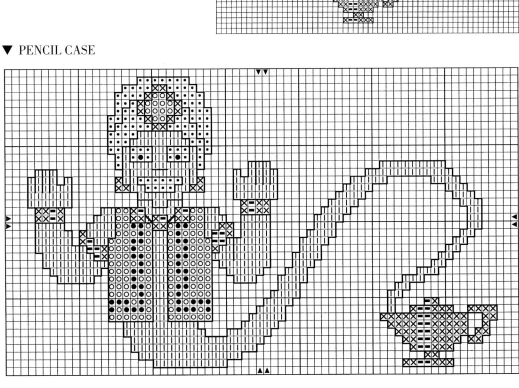

◀ PENCIL CASE
NOVELTIES

GYM BAG ▶

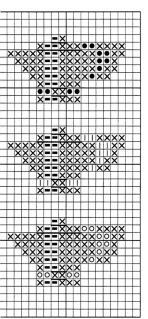

▼ PENCIL CASE

ACKNOWLEDGEMENTS

My grateful thanks go to my family for their invaluable help, and especially to my daughter Elizabeth for her beautiful stitching.

My thanks also go to Coats Paton Crafts for the threads and fabric used in this book and Framecraft Miniatures for the bell pull.

Merehurst would like to thank Hamleys Ltd., London, for lending props for the photographs in this book.

SUPPLIERS

All fabrics and threads were supplied by Coats Paton Crafts (see below) and the bell pull on page 20 was supplied by Framecraft Miniatures Limited, a mail order company that is also a useful source of supply for other cross stitch items, including blank embroidery cards, picture frames and linens:

Framecraft Miniatures Limited
372/376 Summer Lane
Hockley
Birmingham, B19 3QA
England
Telephone: 0121 212 4442

Addresses for Framecraft stockists worldwide
Ireland Needlecraft Pty Ltd
2-4 Keppel Drive
Hallam, Victoria 3803
Australia

Danish Art Needlework
PO Box 442, Lethbridge
Alberta T1J 3Z1
Canada

Sanyei Imports
PO Box 5, Hashima Shi
Gifu 501-62
Japan

The Embroidery Shop
286 Queen Street
Masterton
New Zealand

Anne Brinkley Designs Inc.
246 Walnut Street
Newton
Mass. 02160
USA

S A Threads and Cottons Ltd.
43 Somerset Road
Cape Town
South Africa

For information on your nearest stockist of embroidery cotton, contact the following:

DMC
(also distributors of Zweigart fabrics)

UK
DMC Creative World Limited
62 Pullman Road, Wigston
Leicester, LE8 2DY
Telephone: 0116 2811040

USA
The DMC Corporation
Port Kearney Bld.
10 South Kearney
N.J. 07032-0650
Telephone: 201 589 0606

AUSTRALIA
DMC Needlecraft Pty
P.O. Box 317
Earlswood 2206
NSW 2204
Telephone: 02599 3088

COATS AND ANCHOR
Coats Paton Crafts
McMullen Road
Darlington
Co. Durham DL1 1YQ
Telephone: 01325 381010

USA
Coats & Clark
P.O. Box 27067
Dept CO1
Greenville SC 29616
Telephone: 803 234 0103

AUSTRALIA
Coats Patons Crafts
Thistle Street
Launceston
Tasmania 7250
Telephone: 00344 4222

MADEIRA

UK
Madeira Threads (UK) Limited
Thirsk Industrial Park
York Road, Thirsk
N. Yorkshire, YO7 3BX
Telephone: 01845 524880

USA
Madeira Marketing Limited
600 East 9th Street
Michigan City
IN 46360
Telephone: 219 873 1000

AUSTRALIA
Penguin Threads Pty Limited
25-27 Izett Street
Prahran
Victoria 3181
Telephone: 03529 4400